31 DAYS OF

Self compassion

BY
BLAIR NICOLE, MA IN PSYCHOLOGY

TABLE OF CONTENTS

INTRODUCTION:

mproving your life doesn't come from making monumental changes. You can start exactly where you're at, in whatever situation you're in.

In fact, committing to minor changes each day is far more effective than trying to make huge changes all at once. If you commit to taking small actions each day, over time, these minor changes can lead to massive shifts in your self esteem, confidence, relationships and mental well-being.

My name is Blair Nicole, and I'm a therapist, CEO, author, mom, wife, and traveler. I have a Master's Degree in Psychology, and for the past six years, I've been on a journey of self-discovery, healing from complex trauma, improving my relationships, and learning to love myself.

I know what it's like to feel not good enough. I know what it's like to beat myself up for engaging in the same self-sabotage over and over. I know what it's like to struggle in my relationships. I know what it's like to feel burnt out, exhausted, and at my wits end with trying to manage my life.

Fortunately, somewhere along the way, I learned that the key to improving these areas of my life has been with ME the whole time.

Self compassion.

We have more on our collective plates now than ever before. More expectations and pressure. More social comparisons. More financial strain. More judgment.

And many of us are trying to navigate through these murky waters alone. Talk about an uphill battle!

If you've tried shaming and judging yourself and it didn't work, you're not alone. In fact, shame [1]can lead to more stress, depression, and destruction.

If you've tried to make changes based on pure willpower, you're not alone. If you've tried to make massive changes only to quit a week later, you're not alone.

These methods are ineffective motivators in creating long-term change, and quite frankly, none of them feel great.

Who's ready to try it a different way?

(*Raises hand*)

---

[1] 3 Dangers of shaming. (n.d.). Psychology Today. https://www.psychologytoday.com/us/blog/in-it-together/202103/3-dangers-shaming?eml

Self compassion offers a better way.

According to research[2], there's a link between self-compassion and improved mental and physical health. Practicing self compassion can help us build the internal resources that will not only serve us in tough times, but also help us achieve more of the good times.

If it doesn't come naturally to you, that's okay. It didn't come naturally to me either. That's why it's called a 'practice'.

If you can commit to just five minutes each day - any time of day is fine - you'll be amazed at the changes you see within yourself in a month or a year.

When we choose to put ourselves first, even for five minutes a day, it sends our brains the signal that we're important too! And we are. We are SO important.

You deserve this time for yourself.
You deserve love and kindness.
You deserve joy.
You deserve acceptance.
You deserve self compassion.

I look forward to going on this journey with you.

Blair Nicole

---

[2] Harvard Health. (2024, January 16). The power of self-compassion.
https://www.health.harvard.edu/healthbeat/the-power-of-self-compassion

Disclaimer: The information in this book is not a substitute for medical advice, and it is not intended to diagnose or treat any physical or mental health condition. If you are experiencing a mental health crisis, please contact a licensed mental health professional for support.

DAY 1:

> "Celebrate your wins and forgive yourself for setbacks."

It can be tempting to start any new thing by setting lofty goals, and by picking apart where you've gone wrong in the past.

But, focusing on the problem is never going to get you closer to the solution. It sends your brain the signal that what you've been doing is not good enough. It sends your brain the signal that you need to make radical changes in order to improve your life.

I call BS.

Besides, what kind of energy does that bring into this journey with you?

If there are things you truly don't feel good about, honor that feeling, and then make the radical choice to forgive yourself. Let yourself off the hook. You're doing the best you can with what you've got.

Even if you're not exactly where you want to be right now, I bet there's a whole lot that you ARE getting right.

And, I bet that when you look at all of the things that are going well and choose to celebrate your wins - big and small - you'll get more of the good stuff.

So, start there. You're amazing.

Exercise:

Give yourself permission to acknowledge every little thing that you're doing right. Then, make a list. Write down big things, small things, obscure things. Write down everything.

Did you set a boundary that needed setting? Write it down. Did you show compassion for someone in need? Write it down. Did you take a shower this morning when you would have rather stayed in bed? Let's call that a win!

When you're done, read through your list and allow yourself to feel good about your progress. Sit in those positive feelings for just 1-2 minutes. Notice how your energy shifts.

DAY 2:

"Stop waiting for permission to change. Give yourself full approval to become exactly who you want to be."

You are amazing and beautiful just the way you are. If you never changed another thing about yourself for the rest of your life, you would still be good enough.

That being said, if you're reading this, there are probably a few things in your life that you want to change.

If you've been waiting for someone else's approval or permission to move forward, here's your sign of approval. Go for it. People may not always like or agree to the changes you make, and that's okay. Those are not your people.

If you're ready to evolve, but you've been getting in your own way, that's okay too. When those feelings of fear or procrastination show up, instead of meeting them with judgment and self-loathing, get curious and compassionate instead.

All of us struggle with change. It's human nature to maintain homeostasis. Our brains are quite literally wired to maintain our default settings.

Change is hard. It's uncomfortable. It can be messy. But it's usually worth it.

You were not meant to remain stagnant. You do not have to ask for permission to make the changes you're seeking. You get to live life on your terms.

Exercise:

Take a few slow, deep breaths in through your nose and out through your mouth. Repeat to yourself out loud or in your mind, "I give myself permission to change. It's okay to move forward. It's safe to become exactly the person I want to be."

Sit with this affirmation for 1-2 minutes and notice any feelings that come up. Show yourself compassion for any feelings that are standing in your way. Then, give yourself full permission to move forward anyway.

DAY 3:

> "Be honest with yourself about who you truly want to become. Then, take everything else off the table."

Think of a goal or accomplishment you're working towards. When you think about the goal, do you feel excited or stressed?

If you feel stressed, take a closer look at why you're pursuing it.

Why is that goal important to you? How do you think you'll feel once you've achieved it?

We set goals because we ultimately think we'll feel better when we achieve them. For some of us that feeling might be more peace. For others it might be more joy, more love, more acceptance, more freedom, more safety, or more stability.

Feeling better is almost always the real motive behind any goal you could possibly set.

So, what if that became the goal instead?

It can be easy to give away your energy trying to chase or accomplish things that aren't really what you want. It can also be easy to focus so intently on chasing your goal that you miss opportunities along the way to experience the feeling you're actually seeking!

Ask yourself, what activities and goals are you pursuing that aren't really congruent with the life you're trying to create?

What opportunities are you missing that would allow you to experience more happiness, joy, peace or abundance right now?

Be brutally honest with yourself, and then take the pressure off yourself to accomplish anything that's not in alignment.

Focus on the feelings you want to create more of in your life, and seek out opportunities to increase those feelings right now.

Exercise:

Take a few slow, deep breaths in through your nose and out through your mouth. Ask yourself the question, "What feelings am I truly trying to create in my life?"

Be still while you wait for an answer.

Remember, there's no right or wrong answer. Whatever comes up is totally fine.

Once you have your answer, thank yourself for the insights and affirm to yourself, "I intend to find moments of [whatever feeling you're seeking] today.

Move forward with your day with the intent to tap into that feeling (or feelings) as much as possible.

DAY 4:

"Cut yourself some slack, love. You don't have to figure everything out today."

In a culture that glorifies hustle and burnout, be willing to make the bold choice to cut yourself some slack. It might sound like a radical choice, but it's also one of the most important ones you can make.

It's okay if you don't have everything figured out today.

It's okay to have challenges that don't have solutions yet.

It's okay to take the pressure off...even if it's just for a few hours.

Taking action and showing up is important. But so is taking rest.

When we allow ourselves to rest and step away from our problems, even for a short time, we can prevent burnout and mitigate resentments.

You are a human being deserving of rest and relaxation. You were not put here just to do more stuff and solve more problems. For right now, give yourself permission to just BE.

And the funny thing is, when you allow yourself to rest, recharge, and process, the solutions you've been seeking will often appear...as if out of nowhere.

In stillness you receive so much.

Exercise:

Find a comfortable place to sit or lay down. Close your eyes and affirm to yourself, "It's okay to rest. I give myself permission to relax and recharge. There is nothing I need to do right now. Everything is taken care of."

Allow yourself to rest for 5 minutes with your eyes closed. During this time, focus either on your breath, or on the sounds in the room. When thoughts come up, that's okay. Learning to be still takes practice. Simply notice the thoughts, and then let them go.

By giving yourself just a few minutes to rest, you're reminding yourself that you're important and that it's okay if you don't have all the answers.

DAY 5

"The person you are searching for isn't them.
The person you are searching for is you."

If you've been searching for validation and meaning in something or someone outside of yourself, you have permission to let yourself off the hook.

It happens to the best of us, and it's okay.

You are not wrong for seeking purpose and meaning - these are things that all of us need.

You are not weak for seeking these things in someone else - this is probably just the only way you know how.

Judging yourself for these things is not the path to change. Self-compassion is the way to change.

Recognize that searching for answers in someone else isn't going to work anymore. At the same time, show yourself kindness for the times you forget - you're only human, after all.

Ask yourself what you truly need today - and then give it to yourself.

As you practice non-judgement and self acceptance, you end up becoming the person you've needed all along.

Exercise:

Sit quietly and ask yourself the question, "What do I need today?"

As you do this, take a few slow breaths and try to relax your body.

Once you ask yourself the question, you can take a few minutes of stillness to see what comes up. Or, you can also write the question in a journal, and then allow yourself to write whatever thoughts come up.

If you don't get an answer, or if you start to overthink it, that's okay. Show yourself some grace and compassion if this is difficult. The first step is simply asking yourself the question.

Even if you don't get your answer right away, trust that you intuitively know what you need and that the answer will eventually come to you.

Once you do receive an answer, find ways to give yourself what you need throughout the day. If you need love, give yourself a hug. If you need validation and reassurance, validate and reassure yourself.

Trust that you have the ability to give yourself exactly what you need.

DAY 6

"You can choose to see the good in people, and still recognize their red flags. You can choose to have compassion and still keep your distance. The ability to hold contrasting emotions is a sign of maturity."

You're not 'weak' or 'wrong' for having conflicting feelings about someone. Relationships are complicated, and your feelings don't have to be all-or-nothing.

Being able to hold contrasting emotions can be confusing, but it can also be a sign of emotional maturity.

It's totally okay to love someone, and choose to keep your distance.

It's okay to have empathy and compassion for someone, and still set boundaries around their hurtful behaviors.

Your experience is valid, and you get to decide.

On the other hand, it's also okay to feel anger towards someone and still notice their amazing qualities.

It's okay to be hurt by someone, and choose to keep them in your life anyway because you recognize that they're imperfectly human.

There's no right or wrong answer. Only you know what's best for you.

Allow yourself to have conflicting feelings about people, without trying to contort your emotions into one simple box. When you allow yourself the full range of emotions, the choices you need to make will usually become more clear.

Exercise:

Think about a person or situation that brings up conflicting emotions for you. Notice the feelings that come up, and if possible name each emotion.

Once you've identified the emotions, recognize that each emotion is just a different part of you. All emotions and parts are valid, and all of them are trying to tell you something.

Pick one of the emotions you're feeling, and do your best not to judge it. Instead, get curious about it. Ask that part why it's there and what it's trying to show you. For example, if you notice an angry part and a sad part, you might choose to ask the angry part, "What are you trying to show me? How long have you been there?"

When you receive an answer, thank that part of you and send it some compassion.

Usually you'll come to realize that each emotion is trying to help you or protect you in some way.

If it becomes too difficult to work with the emotion, simply take some slow, relaxing breaths, and bring your mind back to the present.

You can repeat this process with any emotion. The more you're able to get curious about your feelings, the more you'll be able to make choices with clarity.

DAY 7

> "You do not exist just to make someone else happy. You are worthy of love, connection, and joy just because you're you."

You are a worthy human being just because you are you. You deserve love, happiness, connection, and peace with absolutely no strings attached.

You don't have to prove yourself.

You don't have to work for it.

You don't have to sacrifice yourself just to get crumbs of approval and validation in return.

You were not meant to carry around other people's burdens so they don't have to. Leave their burdens to them.

You were not put on this earth for the sole purpose of making someone else happy. You were put here so that YOU could be happy.

You were not put here to become a martyr. You are here so that you can become empowered and fulfilled.

Give yourself the same love and attention that you so freely give to others.

Give it to yourself unconditionally and often.

You're worth it.

Exercise:

Think of the things that make you feel loved and appreciated. Perhaps you feel loved when you're complimented or praised. Maybe you feel loved when someone shows you affection. Or, maybe you feel loved when someone does something nice for you.

There's no right or wrong answer - it's different for everybody. If you're unsure, think about the last time you truly felt loved and appreciated. What happened that brought about those feelings?

Once you have some ideas, start to think of creative ways that you can give those things to yourself today. For example, if affection feels good to you, you can give yourself a hug. If praise is your love language, you can write yourself a love letter. Or if you prefer gifts, you can buy or make yourself a small gift.

You don't have to do anything elaborate. Simply commit to taking one loving act towards yourself, and notice how it feels. You deserve this.

DAY 8

"The point of healing is not just to get better at enduring pain. You've done enough of that."

Learning to sit with uncomfortable feelings is an important part of the healing process. But, healing shouldn't just be a feat of endurance. Healing should be about joy and peace too.

It can be easy to get lost in the trauma, lost in the big emotions, lost in survival mode.

That's understandable. I've been there.

It can also be easy to measure our progress by our ability to handle more shit.

But, let me tell you - that's a trap.

You can only endure so much before you break.

You were not put here just to survive. You're here to thrive.

Realize that it's okay to say no to anything that's causing you more pain. It's okay to opt out of survival mode, even if it's just for today.

Don't forget that healing is also about making space for good things. And you totally deserve the good things.

It's your time to thrive.

Exercise:

What do you need to say no to today?

Recognize the area(s) of your life that are keeping you stuck in survival mode. Notice the things that are preventing you from thriving.

Are there people you need to set boundaries with? Are there things you need to take off your to-do list?

You won't be able to change everything today, and that's okay. But commit to taking one small step.

If you can't think of anything specific, simply take 2-3 minutes to sit in stillness with slow, relaxing breaths. This will send your body the signal that it's safe to come out of survival mode.

DAY 9

"Self-compassion is a practice that takes time to cultivate."

Learning to be kind to yourself takes practice. If you're struggling with self-compassion, try to have compassion for that too.

Self-compassion may not have been taught in your home, and it's rarely reinforced in society. Most of us have decades of conditioning in place that reinforces our inner critic. Making the choice to move forward with compassion is a radical step, and it's going to take some practice.

When you're struggling to find compassion for yourself, or when your inner critic gets loud, try to notice that experience with non judgment.

You're not doing it wrong.

It's not impossible.

It just takes practice, patience, and a bit of un-learning.

Keep making the choice to see yourself with love.

Do it over and over again.

You're heading in the right direction.

Exercise:

When those familiar doubts or self-criticisms come up today, pause and notice them. If you're able to, you can even write them down.

Pretending you don't have those thoughts doesn't help. Healing is not about emotional denial or repression. When we notice our inner critic, we can learn to face it with compassion and kindness.

Simply try not to judge those critical thoughts and feelings. Notice the thoughts, show yourself kindness in the face of them, and then let them go.

Once you've let the feeling go, you open up space to choose new thoughts and beliefs. Ask yourself, "what would I rather believe about myself instead?"

It will take practice and persistence, but this process is super powerful.

DAY 10

> "Asking for help is not a sign of weakness. It's an act of extreme courage, self awareness, and faith."

An important part of self awareness is recognizing when you need help or support. Needing connection and support does not make you weak, dependent, or unhealed. It simply makes you human.

Yes, being able to take care of ourselves is important. But, none of us can do it alone, and healthy connection can help us build resilience. We're social creatures and we need healthy interdependence for survival.

Ultra-independence is often a response to trauma, and not getting our needs met in our relationships.

It's okay to seek connection.

It's okay to ask for help when you need it.

It's okay to be a human being with needs.

Call a friend. Ask for support from family. Hire a therapist. Go to a support group. Lean on your Higher Power.

You don't have to do it alone. You deserve love and support.

Exercise:

Think of an area of your life where you have a hard time allowing help and support. Send yourself love and compassion for all of the times you needed support or connection and didn't get it.

Then, take a deep breath and say to yourself, "It's okay for me to ask for help. I deserve connection and support."

Sit with the feeling for a few minutes and honor any feelings that come up. As you're going through your day, you can return to the affirmation, "It's okay for me to ask for help. I deserve connection and support" as often as you need it.

DAY 11

> "It's okay to love them. Just don't forget to love yourself too."

Love is always the answer. But, don't get so wrapped up in loving someone else that you forget to love yourself too.

Loving someone else does not need to come at the expense of your own safety, sanity, or well-being. Don't give away so much of your energy loving others that you don't have any left for yourself.

Learn to prioritize your own well-being first. Like anything else, it will take practice. You might face some resistance. It will be uncomfortable. You might feel selfish. Do it anyway.

Then, keep on loving people.

Love people when they're struggling.

Love people through their imperfections.

Love people when they make mistakes.

But, don't forget to start with you -

Love yourself when you're struggling.

Love yourself through your imperfections.

Love yourself when you make mistakes.

Love yourself first.

Exercise:

Set aside a few minutes to make a list of everything you like about yourself. Include everything you can possibly think of, even things that seem small or insignificant. Once you've made the list, take two minutes to allow yourself to sit in the feelings of gratitude and appreciation for yourself.

DAY 12

> "Healing begins the moment you give yourself permission to feel and be exactly as you are."

Every emotion serves a purpose, and every feeling tells a story. Feelings are not good or bad; they just are. It's only our beliefs and judgments about certain feelings that keep us trapped.

You are not bad, wrong, or crazy for feeling how you feel. I'm sure whatever you're feeling completely makes sense based on what you've experienced.

So, allow the feeling to just be.

You don't need to ridicule or judge yourself for feeling this way. You don't need to get rid of it.

Get curious about it instead. Where is this feeling coming from? How long have you felt this way? What feelings do you have about the feeling?

When you have the courage to sit with a feeling and ask yourself these questions, you will usually get answers. These answers can lead us to deeper awareness and self compassion.

The paradox is that in accepting how we feel, we also open the door to change.

Exercise:

Set a timer for 3-5 minutes and give yourself permission to just sit with whatever emotion is coming up for you. Notice it, get curious about it, pay attention to where it comes up in your body.

If you start to criticize or judge yourself, notice that too, and then redirect your thoughts back to compassion and curiosity. It's all good.

DAY 13

> "Treat yourself with the same grace and kindness you would give a friend."

You can be your own worst enemy, or your own best friend - the choice is yours.

But, when you choose to be your own best friend instead of beating yourself up, you'll start to feel more supported, centered, and clear-headed. Everything will start to feel more manageable.

If you've been judging yourself or treating yourself poorly, forgive yourself. It happens.

Then, make the radical choice to treat yourself how you would treat a beloved friend or family member.

Would you still love a friend if they messed up?

Would you still support them if they weren't perfect?

Give yourself the same grace and kindness. You deserve it as much as anyone else.

Exercise:

Notice an area of your life where you've been struggling to give yourself grace and kindness. Then, imagine a friend were in your situation, and write 'them' a note offering love and support for what they're going through.

When you're done with the note, read it to yourself and notice how it feels to approach yourself with the same love and kindness.

DAY 14

> "Give yourself the support and compassion you've sought from others and didn't receive."

Maybe you're the one who's always there for everyone else. But, what about you?

Maybe you've spent your life cheerleading and supporting everyone else while expecting nothing in return.

And, truly, that's such an amazing quality.

Being a kindhearted person who shows up for other people is one of your best traits. Don't squash that, babe.

But, don't forget that you need support and compassion too. And, when you don't get that from the people you care most about, it hurts.

If the people you show up for can't show up for you, it's okay to be sad, and it's okay to be angry. That totally makes sense. Give yourself permission to feel all the feels.

Then, give yourself exactly what you've been seeking.

Show up for yourself.

Become your own biggest cheerleader.

Stand in your own corner.

Exercise:

Find a comfortable place to sit for a few minutes. Take a few slow, relaxing breaths in through your nose and out through your mouth.

Repeat this mantra to yourself in your mind or out loud, "I love myself. I support myself. I show up for myself. I know exactly what I need."

Repeat 2-3 times and notice any feelings that show up.

DAY 15

> "You are not your past. You are not your mistakes. You are worthy of forgiveness and healing."

You are a human just like the rest of us, and you don't have to be perfect. You are perfectly imperfect, and mistakes help you learn.

It's common to feel shame, guilt, or judgment towards ourselves when we mess up, but we don't have to live there.

When we get stuck in cycles of judgment and shame, we end up feeling worse and we're more likely to engage in self-sabotaging behavior. It doesn't have to be this way.

You can give yourself permission to let go.

Like so many other things, forgiveness is a process. It's not something that happens all at once. It's something you'll probably have to do multiple times, and that's okay. But, it always begins with a choice.

A choice to see yourself differently.

A choice to give yourself grace.

A choice to free yourself.

Just for today, make the choice to forgive yourself. You deserve it.

Exercise:

Is there something you're having a hard time forgiving yourself for? Are there particular areas of your life where you feel perpetual shame or self-judgment?

As you ask yourself these questions, notice the feelings that come up, and try not to shut them down or repress them. When you notice feelings or shame or judgment, say to yourself "that's okay, it's just a feeling," and imagine sending yourself unconditional love.

Once you've sent yourself love and compassion, make the radical choice to let go.

DAY 16

"There is a season for everything. A season for healing, but also a season for living."

Healing is serious business, but don't get so wrapped up in changing your life that you forget to let yourself live.

What's the point of self-improvement anyway?

To have more joy, more peace, to improve relationships...

And, what's the common denominator in all of these things?

To improve the quality of your LIFE!

So, start today. No matter where you are in your personal journey, give yourself permission to live a little.

Let yourself off the hook.

Don't wait for things to improve before you start living.

The time to start living is now.

Exercise:

Think about what it means to you to truly live. Then, imagine your dream day. Where would you go? What would you do? Who would you spend time with? Get as specific as possible.

Imagine this scenario for 1-2 minutes. Then, ask yourself - what small thing from your ideal life can you actually commit to doing today?

Maybe you can't charter a private yacht around the Greek islands just yet, but perhaps you can get takeout from a new Greek restaurant. Maybe you don't have your dream partner, but you can probably plan a coffee date with a friend who's crazy about you.

Get resourceful and creative, and give yourself full permission to start living today. Even if it's just for 5 minutes at a time.

DAY 17

> "Be the person the unhealed parts of you
> have needed all along."

We all have unhealed wounds - parts of us that are stuck in old stories, old beliefs, and old trauma. This is a normal part of life.

But, when those parts of us go ignored they have the potential to cause chaos in our present life.

Self sabotage. Unhealthy relationship patterns. Addictions and compulsions.

Denying or repressing our unhealed parts may feel compelling in the short term - dealing with painful emotions isn't particularly fun for anyone - but when we ignore our wounds, they tend to just grow deeper.

So, make the choice to lean in.

Make the radical decision today to show up for the parts of you that are unhealed.

Remember, you are capable. You are safe. You are strong. You have everything you need within you to help yourself.

It might be uncomfortable, it might even be a bit painful. But, in doing this, you are creating a sense of safety and trust within yourself.

You can't change the past, but you can show up as the person you need most in the present.

You deserve safety and peace and healing. Start by giving it to yourself.

Set yourself free.

Exercise:

Think of an undesirable situation or pattern in your life that keeps showing up over and over again. Take a minute or two to really sink into the feeling that this situation brings up for you.

Then, ask yourself a few questions:

What part of me needs to heal?

Is there an emotion or belief that I've been avoiding?

How can I show up for this unhealed part?

You may not get the answers you seek right away, but allow yourself to sit in stillness for a couple of minutes, trusting that the answers will come and that you'll know how to show up for yourself.

Imagine sending these unhealed parts of you compassion and acceptance.

DAY 18

"It's okay to be uncomfortable. The change you seek isn't found in your comfort zone."

Becoming the best version of yourself requires a level of discomfort.

Healing requires you to go where you've never gone before, so it makes sense if you feel a bit lost or disoriented.

As humans, it's our natural tendency to try and return things to homeostasis when they change. This is something all of us have in common.

So, give yourself compassion and kindness if you're noticing resistance or fear as you start to make positive changes. This is all part of the process.

Change can be scary. Facing painful emotions can be scary. Going after the things you truly want can be scary.

You're in uncharted territory, babe.

Allow yourself some grace and kindness. And then, boldly continue to move forward anyway.

Exercise:

Sit comfortably and take a few slow, relaxing breaths.

Tell yourself silently or out loud, "It's okay to be uncomfortable. It's okay to be scared. That makes sense. I am safe. It's okay to move forward."

Take a few more slow, relaxing breaths. Slowly clench the muscles in your legs, breathing in as you clench, and exhaling as you release. Notice the sensation of relaxation as you release.

Then, clench the muscles in your abdomen as you breathe in, hold for a moment, and exhale as you release. Notice the feeling of relaxation.

Finally, clench the muscles in your arms, shoulders, and head. Breathe in as you clench, hold for a moment, and then exhale as you release. Notice the feeling of relaxation.

When you're done, repeat to yourself again, "I am safe. It's okay to move forward" as you take a few more slow, relaxing breaths.

DAY 19

> "Trust yourself, and trust the process. Everything is working out exactly as it should be."

Life won't always go according to plan. Sometimes things will feel uncertain, chaotic, or downright awful.

Let it be.

Wherever you're at right now, send yourself compassion and remind yourself that ups and downs are all part of the process.

It can be hard to trust that things will work out. But, you've made it this far!

You are strong. You are resilient. You know how to show up for yourself. You can face the ups and downs of life and still be okay.

When things feel like they're falling apart, choose to trust yourself. You are your own greatest asset.

You've got this.

Exercise:

Make a list of all of the times you've made decisions you're proud of, times you've felt accomplished, and times things have worked out for you.

Be sure to include big decisions, small decisions, and everything in between. The goal is to make a list of experiences that exemplify that you're trustworthy and capable.

Write this list in your journal or somewhere you can look at it again when you're struggling with uncertainty or self-doubt.

When you're done writing the list, spend 1-2 minutes noticing the feelings of trust and self-confidence.

DAY 20

> "You don't have to be perfect, babe. It's okay to be human."

Perfectionism is a liability, not an asset.

It will not make you stronger, more successful, or immune to vulnerability. It might feel like a well-worn shield that protects you from failure and rejection, but that's merely an illusion.

Here's the truth - holding yourself to unrealistic standards is getting in the way of you living your best life.

Perfectionism begets shame and isolation, and a constant pressure to perform. These things keep us stuck and disconnected...from ourselves and each other.

If that's where you're at, don't beat yourself up. I've been there too.

Instead, make the radical choice to send yourself compassion. These are feelings we all experience from time to time, and they're not something you need to hide from.

But, you also don't need to cling to these expectations of yourself. You are free to let that shit go.

It's okay to make mistakes.

It's okay to be imperfect.

It's okay to feel exactly how you feel.

It's okay to try and fail.

It's okay to try and succeed.

It's absolutely, positively okay to be YOU.

Exercise:

Think of a situation where you're holding yourself to an unreasonable standard, or expecting perfection from yourself.

Then, ask yourself, "What would happen if I stopped holding myself to this standard? What would happen if I let myself show up imperfectly?"

It's okay if you notice some fear or resistance. That's a common response. Send yourself compassion for whatever thoughts or feelings come up.

You probably won't be able to change your perspective overnight, and that's to be expected. You've probably held these beliefs for quite some time.

The point of this exercise is to recognize that nothing catastrophic will happen if you don't show up perfectly. Through this exercise you might also realize that your expectations of yourself stem from past beliefs or experiences. Once you recognize this, you can begin to choose whether or not we want to change your perspective.

As you go through this exercise, keep coming back to a stance of compassion and non-judgment towards yourself no matter what comes up.

DAY 21

> "It's okay if things aren't going according to plan. What if this detour ends up being one of the best things you never saw coming?"

Things won't always go according to your plans.

When this happens, allow things to go wrong.

Don't burn yourself out trying to resist the reality of the situation.

Don't beat yourself up about it.

And, don't get so caught up in clinging to your plan that you miss the opportunities in front of you right now.

It makes sense that you're disappointed. It makes sense that the detour is frustrating. It makes sense that you're scared.

Be kind to yourself as you adjust to the reality of the situation. But, don't fight it. Allow yourself to accept things just as they are.

Acceptance paves the way for you to move forward.

Exercise:

Take a few minutes to reflect on how you respond when things don't go according to plan. Do you allow things to unfold? Or, do you spend your energy trying to force things?

Approach yourself with curiosity and compassion. If you notice self-judgments or criticisms, that's okay - simply notice what comes up and then return to compassion. It's all good.

Then, take a few slow, relaxing breaths in through your nose and out through your mouth, as you repeat to yourself, "I accept things as they are. I accept myself as I am."

DAY 22

> "You are enough."

You are good enough exactly as you are.

You don't have to prove to anyone else that you're worthy, because you already are.

If someone has hurt you, be gentle with yourself. Know in your heart that you didn't deserve the hurt that you received.

Then, remind yourself - other people's opinions and choices have nothing to do with you. These things are merely a reflection of their own internal struggles. Yes, those struggles might hurt you. But they're never really about you.

If something in your life has made you doubt yourself, realize that this, too, is a normal part of life. We all have self doubts. It's our choice whether we want to cling to them, or love ourselves in spite of them.

No matter what has happened, you are good enough.

Even on your worst days, you are good enough.

You always have been, and you always will be.

Exercise:

Make a list of 3-5 things you truly like or appreciate about yourself. It doesn't matter what you put on the list, as long as they're things that you can truly connect with.

Then, take a few slow, relaxing breaths and repeat the following affirmation, using the list you just created:

"I am enough.

I like that I am (repeat something from your list)...

I like that I am (repeat something from your list)...

I like that I am (repeat something from your list)...

I am enough."

DAY 23

"When all else fails, have fun."

If you've been stuck in a rut, or if life has become mundane, this is your sign that it's time to lighten up. The struggle may be real, but life is meant to be enjoyed.

I know that it can be hard to lighten up when things seem so challenging.

If you're facing hardships or setbacks, send yourself compassion for the struggles you're facing. Then, make the radical choice to approach them with lightness anyway.

The challenges will still be there at the end of the day, love. So, you might as well have some fun while you're at it. It's not irresponsible or immature.

It's not frivolous.

Having fun is absolutely necessary.

Tell yourself that it's safe to let go of the seriousness just for today.
Your biggest breakthroughs and creative inspirations will often come from allowing yourself a break to play and be joyful.

Exercise:

Think of a situation in your life that you've been taking very seriously. What would it be like if you approached this situation with more fun and lightheartedness? How would your experience change if you allowed yourself to have more fun?

Notice if any feelings of resistance come up when you think about approaching this situation with fun and lightheartedness. Approach yourself with non-judgment and compassion.

Then, choose one small thing you can do today to have fun, even if it's only for a few minutes.

DAY 24

> "It's okay to not be okay. Allow yourself to be exactly as you are."

Whatever you're feeling today is okay. Send yourself the ultimate message of self-acceptance by allowing yourself to be exactly as you are.

Your feelings don't have to be justified. They don't even have to make sense. Just for today, feel all the feels without judgment.

If you notice resistance, send yourself compassion and then make space for the feelings anyway. What you resist will persist.

Keep in mind that feelings aren't good or bad. It's only your beliefs and judgments about them that give them power.

It's okay to feel happy. It's okay to feel sad.

It's okay to feel angry. It's okay to feel despair.

It's okay to feel jealous. It's okay to feel okay.

It's important to remember that feelings are also different from behaviors. For example, you can feel intense anger without choosing to take your anger out on someone. Allow the feelings to come without the need to act them out as behaviors. This will probably take some practice, and that's okay. Today is a great day to get started.

Exercise:

Find a safe space where you can get comfortable. Set a timer for 5 minutes and allow yourself to truly feel whatever you're feeling during that time.

Remind yourself that there are no bad feelings and that it's safe to allow whatever comes up.

If you notice fear or judgment, take a few slow, relaxing breaths and send yourself kindness and compassion. This process can be difficult.

When you're done, thank yourself for taking the time to do this. Then, take a few moments to slow your breathing and relax your body before you continue your day.

DAY 25

"The present moment is the most powerful place you can be."

The most important thing you can do for yourself today is to be present. The power to change always starts here and now.

When things become challenging or mundane, it becomes all-too-easy to go through our days in a daze. We get stuck doing the same things over and over again, physically present but mentally and spiritually asleep. Then, before we know it, another year has passed and nothing has changed.

If this sounds familiar, don't beat yourself up. It's a natural human tendency, and we've all been there.

But let this also serve as a reminder - today holds the potential for amazing things if you choose to be present.

Don't sleepwalk through today, or you'll miss all of the good stuff. You'll miss important connections, opportunities, lessons, and magical moments that you'll never get back.

Most importantly, you'll miss the opportunity to truly connect with yourself.

So, just for today, make the decision -

Be here now.

Exercise:

Take a few slow, deep breaths and relax your body as much as possible. Take a few moments to look around the room you're sitting in.

Try to notice new and different things about the stuff in your environment that has become ordinary. Notice what you can see, what you can hear, what you can touch, what you can smell. Tune into your five senses and just notice what comes up.

As you do this exercise, it not only helps you to become mindful and present, but it also trains your brain to see ordinary things in a new way.

DAY 26

> "Love yourself exactly the way you want to be loved. Everything and everyone else will follow suit."

The quality of the love you receive always begins with the quality of love you give yourself.

This may be a hard and uncomfortable truth.

If you've never been loved unconditionally, or if you've experienced neglect, abuse, or trauma, it can be really hard to love yourself. Without a model for unconditional love, you may not know where to start. That's okay, I've been there too. Send yourself love and compassion for all of the love you wanted and didn't receive.

But then, commit to loving yourself the way you've always wanted to be loved.

It will take practice.

It probably won't come naturally.

You will be tempted to fall back into old habits and beliefs.

All of this is part of the process.

When these things happen, notice them, reassure yourself that it's all okay, and then send yourself as much love as you possibly can in that moment.

Self-love is a practice, and it takes time. But, you are absolutely worth it.

You have deserved unconditional love all along, and it's time to claim what's yours.

Exercise:

Take a few slow, deep breaths and relax your body as much as possible. Imagine yourself as a child or adolescent. Whatever age comes to mind first is perfectly fine.

Once you have an image of yourself as a child, ask that child what they want or need most from you.

Try your best not to judge any responses that come up. Instead try to give the child what they need from you. Maybe they need love and acceptance, maybe they need safety and protection, or maybe they need something else entirely.

There are no right or wrong answers, this is simply a curious inquiry that will help you learn to know and love yourself better.

When you're done, thank the child for sharing with you, and then send yourself love and compassion as you head into your day.

DAY 27

> "Approach your day with curiosity. Learn to ask questions, and you'll start to get answers."

When was the last time you paused to ask yourself why you feel a certain way or why you keep doing certain things?

Awareness is the first step towards empowerment and change. But first, you must have the courage to get curious about yourself.

It can be uncomfortable, and it can lead to more questions. But it will also lead you back to your true self.

Your thoughts, feelings, beliefs, and behaviors are not static. Nothing is set in stone. Everything in your life is malleable and overcomeable - you just have to be open to getting curious about it first.

Get curious about yourself. Get curious about your feelings, your patterns, and your beliefs. Get curious about the situations in your life that are challenging.

When you adopt an attitude of curiosity, rather than judgment, the answers you've been seeking will start to show up. Be gentle and patient. Some answers might surprise you, and that's okay. It's all part of the journey.

By getting curious, you're giving yourself the gift of understanding, self-compassion, and, ultimately, the power to change.

Exercise:

As you go through your day, try to notice when habitual feelings, thoughts, or behaviors come up. When that happens, approach them with curiosity. Begin to ask yourself why you feel a certain why, or why you do a certain thing. It might help to write things down as you notice them.

Don't judge anything that comes up, just observe and get curious. If judgment does come up, forgive yourself and then let the judgment go, so you can return to a place of self-compassion.

This exercise will help you build a deeper relationship with yourself.

DAY 28

> "Sometimes you'll want to give up, and that's okay. Give yourself permission to rest, and then start again."

I know it's hard to admit that you need a break. You've got so much on your plate, after all.

But, if you don't allow yourself to rest and recharge now, life will find some other way to remind you that you need to slow down. And usually those reminders aren't very fun.

When you feel like giving up, your instincts might tell you to push harder. But, what if that's not what you actually need?

In times like these, what you probably need the most is a break.

I know that it might seem counterintuitive.

It might feel uncomfortable.

It might even feel scary to step away from things right now.

But, you're a human being and human beings need to rest and recharge from time to time. There's no shame in that.

So, if you've started to feel overwhelmed, exhausted, or hopeless, give yourself permission to take a much needed respite.

The responsibilities and challenges will still be there when you return, and you'll probably be in a much better headspace to deal with them. Most things seem more manageable after a nap, a hot shower, or simply taking a few hours off.

Give yourself a break, babe. And when you're done resting, go back to being your usual badass self.

Exercise:

Take a moment to ask yourself if you're feeling burnt out, exhausted, hopeless, or overwhelmed.

If the answer is yes, commit to giving yourself a mini-break from the stress today. Even if it's just 5-10 minutes, allow yourself to unplug, step away, and just let it all go.

If you notice resistance, remind yourself, "It's safe to step away. It's safe to relax right now."

Even if you're not feeling burnt out or overwhelmed right now, still give yourself 5-10 minutes to step away and relax today. The best way to avoid burnout is to be proactive in taking care of yourself.

DAY 29

"Let it go. Don't cling to things that are not serving you."

You might think you're protecting yourself by clinging to certain feelings or behaviors, but what you're actually doing is keeping yourself stuck.

I get it. I've been there myself.

If you've experienced trauma or loss, it can be hard to let go of things like fear, anger, anxiety, and resentment. And, considering what you've been through, it totally makes sense. Hanging on to these things protects you, after all. By staying angry, anxious, afraid, and resentful, you build walls around yourself that safeguard you from more rejection, loss and abandonment.

But, by hanging on to these things, you also shield yourself from growth, connection, healing, and opportunity. These things are the best parts of life.

It's time to allow more for yourself. It's time to let that shit go.

I know it can feel risky and vulnerable to let go. Trust that you can handle the risk.

Trust that things will probably work out. And, that you can handle it even if they don't.

Letting go is both a choice and a habit.

First you make the choice to move forward.

Then, you make the choice over and over again until it becomes easy.

And, I promise It will get easier.

Letting go will offer you the freedom and opportunities you so deserve.

Exercise:

If you've been struggling to let go of habits, beliefs or feelings that no longer serve you - first, make the radical choice to forgive yourself. You've done the best you can with the resources you've had at your disposal.

Tell yourself, "I forgive myself for doing what I had to do to protect myself. I forgive myself for hanging on to things that don't serve me."

Then, take a few slow deep breaths and relax your body as much as possible. Tell yourself, "I am willing to let go. It's safe to let go now."

As you go through this process, remind yourself that letting go won't happen overnight. The old feelings and habits will come up again, and that's okay. It happens to everyone.

When you notice that you're clinging to things that don't serve you, notice it, and then release it. Send yourself as much compassion as possible through this process.

DAY 30

> "You are doing the best you can with what you've got. Progress will continue to beget more progress."

The old saying "practice makes perfect" was obviously not written about humans. It's also complete and utter bullshit.

Even the most enlightened, intelligent, and altruistic people among us are far from perfect. Making mistakes is part of the learning and growing process.

It's interesting how we offer so much grace and kindness to young children who are learning to do things for the first time. We inherently know that they're doing the best they can, and that they'll eventually figure it out as long as they keep trying.

What if you offered that same attitude towards yourself? Imagine the possibilities!

You do not have to be perfect. It's okay to mess up. It's okay to get things wrong the first ten (or one hundred) times. Forgive yourself and move on. You're learning, and you're growing, and that's the important part.

Notice the progress you have made, and celebrate small wins along the way. Any progress you make will become a stepping stone for more progress.

No matter what you're going through, remind yourself that you're doing the best you can with what you've got. And as you continue to learn and grow, things will get better and better.

You're doing a great job. You've got this.

Exercise:

Take a few minutes to write down any accomplishments or signs of progress you've noticed in yourself over the past year. It doesn't matter how big or small they are, just write them down.

When you're done with the list, take 1-2 minutes to sit with the feelings of accomplishment and progress. Notice how it feels in your body, notice how your mood shifts. Really pay attention to what this feels like.

Make a choice to return to these feelings of accomplishment and progress any time you start to doubt yourself.

DAY 31

"The way you speak about yourself matters. You will always follow through on who you believe you are."

What you believe about yourself shapes your identity, your relationships, and your life.

I know that things are not always fair, and that life circumstances are a contributing factor in your success and happiness. You may have experienced trauma, marginalization, or loss that has made things more difficult for you. You didn't deserve these things, and they're not your fault.

But, regardless of what's happened in the past, you have a choice today to decide what you want to believe about yourself. What you believe about yourself will always, always predict how you show up in the world.

If you believe you're flawed, not good enough, or broken, you will continue to choose thoughts, relationships, and behaviors to prove yourself right. For better or for worse, your beliefs create self-fulfilling prophecies.

It's a natural human tendency to seek out information that confirms what we already believe to be true. It happens to all of us.

So, if this sounds like you, you're off the hook. There's no need to beat yourself up, babe.

The good news is, you also have the power to change how you see yourself.

By practicing self awareness, you can notice those un-helpful core beliefs when they come up, get curious about them, and then let them go. When you do this, you have the power to choose new beliefs that truly serve you.

Who do you most want to be? What do you want to believe about yourself? How do you want to show up in the world?

You have the ultimate authority over who you become.

But, first you must decide.

Exercise:

Find a quiet place to sit, and take a few slow, relaxing breaths. Ask yourself, "Who do I most want to be? What do I want to believe about myself?" Don't judge the answers that come up, simply notice them.

As answers start to come up, consider how your day would be different if you already believed those things about yourself. For example, if you want to believe that you're good with money, and great at maintaining healthy relationships, you would start to ask yourself what it would feel like if you already believed those things about yourself.

Then, find moments during the day to act as if those beliefs were already true.

ADDITIONAL RESOURCES & CONNECT WITH ME

Thank you so much for allowing me to share this journey with you. I hope you found the ideas and exercises in this book to be helpful.

If you want to keep the momentum going, you might also enjoy the free download I've created just for you:

"One Week of Meditation and Journaling to Increase Self-Love"

You'll get 7 more days of inspiration that will help you meditate and journal your way to self compassion, self confidence, and self acceptance.

Download it for free here:
https://blairnicole.blog/selflovefreedownload

In addition to the free download, you can also connect with me via the resources below:

- Website / Blog: https://blairnicole.blog/

- Instagram:
  https://www.instagram.com/officialblairnicole/

- Book a Coaching Consultation:
  https://calendly.com/mediamogulspr/30-minute-coaching-consultation

Printed in Great Britain
by Amazon

60878526R00047